G

Sports

Contents

Features

Sports news is a big part of the daily news on television, on the radio and in the newspapers. Read **In the News** for some sporting stories.

Which word, made up in the 1950s, is the name of a special event for athletes with physical disabilities? Find out on page 15.

How many times a week does swimmer Ian Thorpe train? Read his training schedule on page 19 and see if you could keep up!

Shannon Miller was the first American to win a gold medal for her specialty event. Turn to page 25 to find out what that event was.

What are the different swimming strokes?

Visit www.infosteps.co.uk
for more about **SPORTS**.

Good Sports

Today top athletes are often well known by thousands of people around the world. They are admired by fans for their physical strengths and their skills. Sports stars such as Pelé, Tracey Ferguson, Ian Thorpe, and Shannon Miller have made outstanding performances during their sporting careers. As well as being skilled in a sport, a lot of hard work in both training and practising is behind their successes.

You don't have to be a star, however, to enjoy playing a sport. Like any top athlete you too can set and achieve goals, train, practise and be successful in your sport.

Key to Athletes

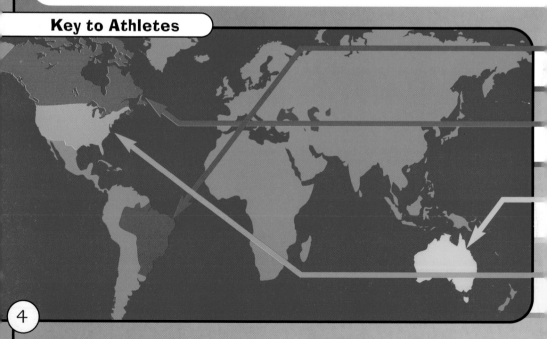

Sport is played for fun, exercise, competition and achievement. Training and practising helps achieve success in sport.

Pelé, Brazil, soccer

Tracey Ferguson, Canada, wheelchair basketball

Ian Thorpe, Australia, swimming

Shannon Miller, United States, gymnastics

Pelé

Who Is Pelé?

Pelé, whose real name is Edson Arantes do Nascimento, was born in 1940 in a small Brazilian village. His first job was shining shoes. However, he had dreamed of playing soccer since he was a young boy.

At the age of just thirteen Pelé was discovered by former Brazilian World Cup player Waldemar de Brito. De Brito asked Pelé to join his team. In 1956 de Brito took Pelé to try out for the Santos Football Club in Sao Paulo. When Pelé was invited to join the team his soccer career began. De Brito told the team directors, "This boy will be the greatest soccer player in the world."

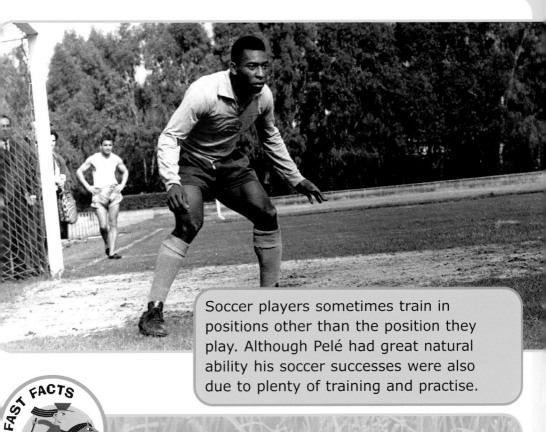

Soccer players sometimes train in positions other than the position they play. Although Pelé had great natural ability his soccer successes were also due to plenty of training and practise.

FAST FACTS

Pelé's Records

As well as holding every major scoring record in Brazil Pelé also holds the following records:

• Most goals in a career: 1,281 in 1,363 games between 1956 and 1977

• Only player to have been on three World Cup-winning teams: 1958, 1962, 1970

• Youngest scorer in a World Cup final match: 17 years, 239 days old on June 19, 1958 against Wales

Pelé became well known when he was seventeen years old and playing for the Santos club in Brazil. He helped lead Brazil to its first World Cup win in 1958. He led the team to victory in the World Cup again in 1962 and in 1970. Pelé retired from the Brazilian national team in 1971 and from his club team in 1974. From 1975 to 1977 Pelé played for the New York Cosmos in the United States.

Apart from his expert skills on the soccer field Pelé is known for his friendly personality and his love of teaching the game. He is still thought of around the world as the greatest soccer player of all time.

Pelé moved to the United States in 1975 to play for the New York Cosmos and to promote the game of soccer. At the time soccer wasn't well known in the USA. After two years of Pelé's work the number of registered soccer players had increased from 100,000 to 400,000.

Pelé played for the Brazilian national team from 1958 until 1971. He led the team to victory in the World Cup three times.

Sports News December 17, 2002

2002 King and Queen of Soccer

Soccer's king and queen for 2002 have been named by the official soccer world governing body, the FIFA.

Mia Hamm, of the United States national soccer team, was named Women's World Player of the Year, and Ronaldo, Brazilian World Cup soccer star, was named Men's World Player of the Year. Mia also won the award in 2001 when it was given for the first time.

Mia was unable to play for the first half of the 2002 season due to knee surgery, however, she still kicked a huge number of goals over the remainder of the season. Mia only played in nine matches, but finished fourth on the team with seven goals.

Ronaldo and Mia Hamm, winners of the 2002 World Soccer Player of the Year awards

Walter Payton (1954–1999)

The Chicago Bears football team has lost one of its most valued former players. Walter Payton died at his home in South Barrington, Illinois today at age 45. In his thirteen-year career as a running back Walter averaged 1,337 yards rushing per season. He missed only one game in his entire career and that was in his **rookie** year.

To his millions of fans in Chicago and around the world Walter was known as "Sweetness". He earned this name both for the way he played on the field and for his behaviour off the field. After retiring from football Walter ran his own business. He also set up the Walter Payton Foundation to help disadvantaged children in Illinois and other parts of the United States.

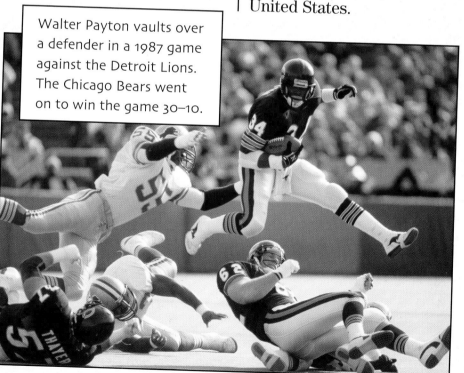

Walter Payton vaults over a defender in a 1987 game against the Detroit Lions. The Chicago Bears went on to win the game 30–10.

Tracey Ferguson

Who Is Tracey Ferguson?

Tracey Ferguson was born in Ontario, Canada in 1974. At the age of eleven she joined a sports and fitness centre in Toronto and signed up for wheelchair basketball, wheelchair tennis and wheelchair racing.

At first Tracey found basketball very difficult. She was the only female player, she was very small and she couldn't shoot a basket. However, her love of the game made her very determined to succeed. Today Tracey is still one of the smallest players in the world, but she overcomes this with speed, **agility** and expert shooting.

Tracey played for the University of Illinois team when she was studying in the United States.

What Is a "Professional"?

Professional athletes are paid to train, practise and play their sport. Amateur athletes are not paid. However, the cost of living, training and travelling is very high for many athletes. At first only amateur athletes were permitted to compete in the Olympic or Paralympic Games. Today some sports in the Games allow athletes to have some of their expenses paid by governments or **sponsors.**

Tracey is one of the smaller players on the Canadian team. She is pictured above (in the front row, fourth from the left) after winning the 1998 World Wheelchair Basketball Championships held in Sydney, Australia.

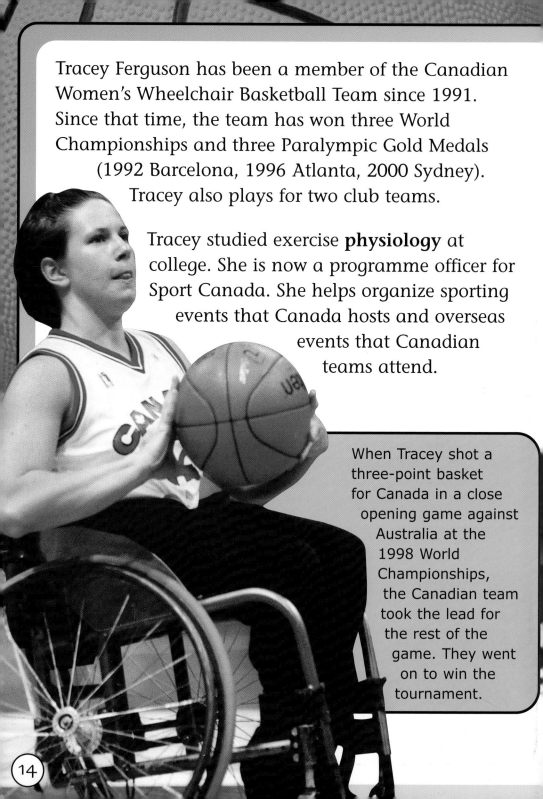

Tracey Ferguson has been a member of the Canadian Women's Wheelchair Basketball Team since 1991. Since that time, the team has won three World Championships and three Paralympic Gold Medals (1992 Barcelona, 1996 Atlanta, 2000 Sydney). Tracey also plays for two club teams.

Tracey studied exercise **physiology** at college. She is now a programme officer for Sport Canada. She helps organize sporting events that Canada hosts and overseas events that Canadian teams attend.

When Tracey shot a three-point basket for Canada in a close opening game against Australia at the 1998 World Championships, the Canadian team took the lead for the rest of the game. They went on to win the tournament.

Tracey believes that basketball has given her much more than just medals and championships. She has gained a healthy lifestyle, high **self-esteem** and many friendships. Tracey often speaks to groups of school children. She hopes to teach them the benefits of sport and being active in their lives.

Tracey holds the Gold Cup after winning the 1998 World Wheelchair Basketball Championships held in Sydney, Australia.

WORD BUILDER

Paralympic Games

Many people think that the word *paralympic* comes from the words *paraplegic* and *Olympic*. In fact the word *para* is from the Greek language and means "alongside". Both the summer and winter Paralympic Games, for people with physical disabilities, are held in the same location two weeks after, or "alongside", the Olympic Games.

Paralympic Performances

Sports News   March 15, 2002

Speed at Snowbasin

Australian skier Bart Bunting has won three medals in three different events at the winter Paralympic Games held in Salt Lake City, Utah. This is an amazing achievement, especially since Bart is totally blind. He won gold for both the downhill and super *G* skiing events and silver in the giant slalom.

Although Bart has always been active in many sports including the triathlon, rock climbing and canoeing, he skied for the first time only four years ago.

Bart credits a lot of his success to always having the same ski guide, long-time friend Nathan Chivers. When they're racing Bart and Nathan communicate through radio headsets. Nathan calls out instructions such as "left", "right", "straight" or "icy".

This is obviously a team that works well together.

Left: Bart in action
Below: Nathan leads Bart to gold in the super *G* event

Three Times a Winner

Louise Sauvage, of Australia, has won the wheelchair division of the Boston Marathon for the third year running. It was another close finish, but not as close as her 1998 win. That race featured the closest finish in the history of the marathon. As leader Jean Driscoll started to lift her arms to go through the tape Louise surged ahead in the final second to win. The finish was so close that both women recorded a time of one hour, 41 minutes and 19 seconds.

Louise Sauvage and Jean Driscoll congratulate each other in 1998.

Louise is no stranger to racing. She got her first racing chair at the age of eight. She competed in her first major road race when she was nineteen and began racing seriously a year later. She is now training for the 2000 Sydney Olympic Games.

Ian Thorpe

Who Is Ian Thorpe?

Ian Thorpe was born in Sydney, Australia in 1982. As a young child he enjoyed many sports, including cricket, rugby league and soccer. He learned to swim at an early age, but didn't begin training until he was eight years old. After watching his older sister compete at swimming carnivals he decided he'd like to compete too.

At fourteen Ian became the youngest male to qualify for the Australian swimming team. As a member of this team he won two silver medals at the Pan Pacific Championships in Japan. A year later he won his first gold medal for the 400-metre freestyle at the World Championships.

What are the different swimming strokes?

Visit **www.infosteps.co.uk**
for more about **SPORTS.**

APRIL 2003

Week 15 : 97-268

7 Monday

Training 5:00AM–7:30AM

Training 4:00PM–6:00PM

Week 15 : 98-267

8 Tuesday

Training 5:00AM–7:30AM

Training 4:00PM–6:00PM

Week 15 : 99-266

9 Wednesday

Sleep In

Training 4:00PM–6:00PM

Week 15 : 100-265

10 Thursday

Training 5:00AM–7:30AM

Training 4:00PM–6:00PM

APRIL 2003

Week 15 : 101-264

Friday 11

Training 5:00AM–7:30AM

Training 4:00PM–6:00PM

Week 15 : 102-263

Saturday 12

Training 5:00AM–7:30AM

Afternoon Free

Week 15 : 103-262

Sunday 13

Rest Day!

April 2003						
M		7	14	21	28	
T	1	8	15	22	29	
W	2	9	16	23	30	
T	3	10	17	24		
F	4	11	18	25		
S	5	12	19	26		
S	6	13	20	27		

May 2003						
M		5	12	19	26	
T		6	13	20	27	
W		7	14	21	28	
T	1	8	15	22	29	
F	2	9	16	23	30	
S	3	10	17	24	31	
S	4	11	18	25		

IN FOCUS

Training Schedule

Ian Thorpe trains in the pool ten times a week. He also has two weight-training sessions and two boxing sessions per week.

Ian Thorpe became well known worldwide after his outstanding performance at the 2000 Sydney Olympic Games—his first Olympic Games appearance. On Day One of the games he won Australia's first gold medal with a world-record swim in the 400-metre freestyle.

Only an hour later he swam the final leg of the 4 x 100-metre freestyle relay, winning gold and setting yet another world record.

Ian Thorpe finished his first Olympic Games with three gold medals and two silver medals. He was also given the honour of carrying Australia's flag at the closing ceremony.

Career Time Line

1990—Ian begins swimming training.

1994—Ian joins coach Doug Frost and moves to a senior squad.

1997—Ian is selected for the Australian national team.

1997—Ian wins two silver medals at the Pan Pacific Championships (Japan).

1998—Ian wins four gold medals at the Commonwealth Games in Kuala Lumpur.

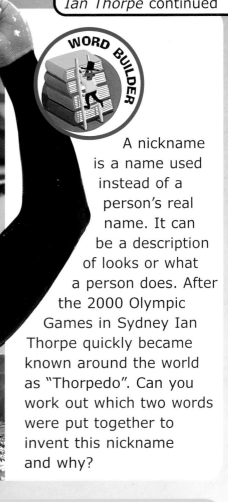

WORD BUILDER

A nickname is a name used instead of a person's real name. It can be a description of looks or what a person does. After the 2000 Olympic Games in Sydney Ian Thorpe quickly became known around the world as "Thorpedo". Can you work out which two words were put together to invent this nickname and why?

1999—Ian breaks four world records in four days at the Pan Pacific Championships (Australia).

2000—Ian wins three gold and two silver medals at the Sydney Olympic Games.

2001—In the World Championships Ian wins six gold medals and breaks four world records.

2003—At the World Cup Ian swims the second-fastest 200-metre freestyle ever recorded.

Swimming Successes

Sports News   **September 12, 1972**

Seven Gold Medals, Seven World Records

Shane Gould

Munich, West Germany

American swimmer Mark Spitz has won more gold medals than any other Olympian in the history of the Olympic Games. He won all four of his individual events—the 100-metre and 200-metre freestyle, the 100-metre and 200-metre butterfly—and all his relay events. As well as winning gold for all seven events he set a new world record in each of the seven races.

While Mark Spitz is the star of the men's swimming events Australian swimmer Shane Gould is the star of the women's events. At just fifteen years old she has won five individual medals at these Games—three gold, one silver and one bronze. She has also set three new world records in the 200-metre and 400-metre freestyle and the 200-metre individual medley.

Left: Mark Spitz swims for gold at the Munich Olympic Games in 1972.

New Record at Sydney Olympics

Eric Moussambani, also known as Eric the Eel, has become the accidental hero of the 2000 Sydney Olympic Games. Eric's new record, however, is a little different from most records set at Olympic events. His record is for swimming very, very slowly. Eric, of Equatorial Guinea, just learned how to swim in January this year.

His fellow competitors were **disqualified** from his heat and Eric had to swim the 100-metre race alone. He nearly didn't make it to the end of the race, but with a large crowd cheering him on he finished in a time of one minute, 52 seconds. This time is a minute slower than the times of the other heat winners.

Shannon Miller

Who Is Shannon Miller?

Shannon Miller is a US gymnast who was born in Missouri in 1977. During her sporting career she won more Olympic and World Championship medals than any other American gymnast in history. In an international career that began in 1990 Shannon won seven Olympic medals and nine World Championship medals.

While Shannon's specialty was the balance beam she also competed in the vault, floor exercises and the uneven parallel bars.

Throughout her career Shannon won a total of 59 international medals (over half of these were gold) and 49 national medals (again, over half of these were gold). In 1994 she became the only American gymnast to win world titles two years running.

FAST FACTS

Shannon Miller was the first American to win a gold medal on the balance beam. The balance beam is a long thin beam that is 10 centimetres wide. Competitors try to use its full length doing leaps, jumps, running steps and turns on it. The routine must last between 70 and 90 seconds. Top competitors like Shannon also perform handsprings and somersaults.

As well as being famous for winning so many medals Shannon Miller is well known for her determined goal setting and her leadership qualities. Her leadership skills were very clear at the 1996 Olympic Games where she led the United States Women's Gymnastics Team to its first gold medal. At the same Games she became the first American to win gold for her performance on the balance beam.

Shannon officially retired from gymnastics in December 2001. Today Shannon enjoys talking with students at gymnastics camps and at colleges throughout the United States about goal setting and **motivation**.

At the 1996 Olympic Games held in Atlanta, Georgia the women's team from the United States won gold in the Women's Team Gymnastics competition. Pictured on the winners' **podium** are, from left to right, Dominique Moceanu, Kerri Strug and Shannon Miller.

A strong and steady finishing position is important for gaining high points.

The floor exercise is performed to music. Gymnasts demonstrate their skills in acrobatics, dancing and tumbling in time with the music.

27

The Best Sports

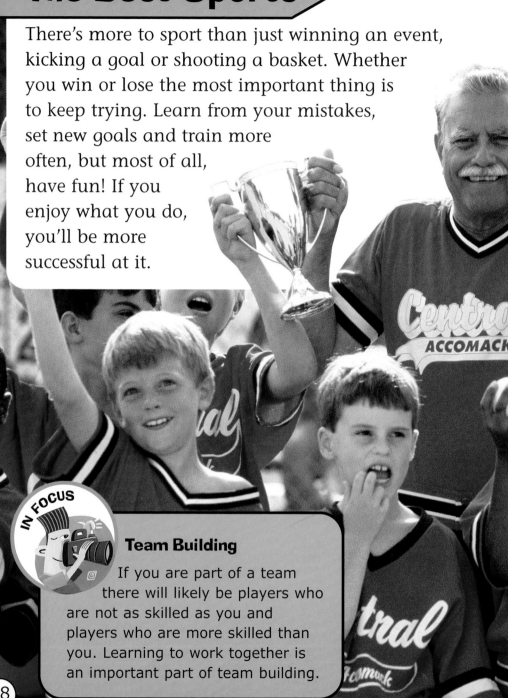

There's more to sport than just winning an event, kicking a goal or shooting a basket. Whether you win or lose the most important thing is to keep trying. Learn from your mistakes, set new goals and train more often, but most of all, have fun! If you enjoy what you do, you'll be more successful at it.

Team Building

If you are part of a team there will likely be players who are not as skilled as you and players who are more skilled than you. Learning to work together is an important part of team building.

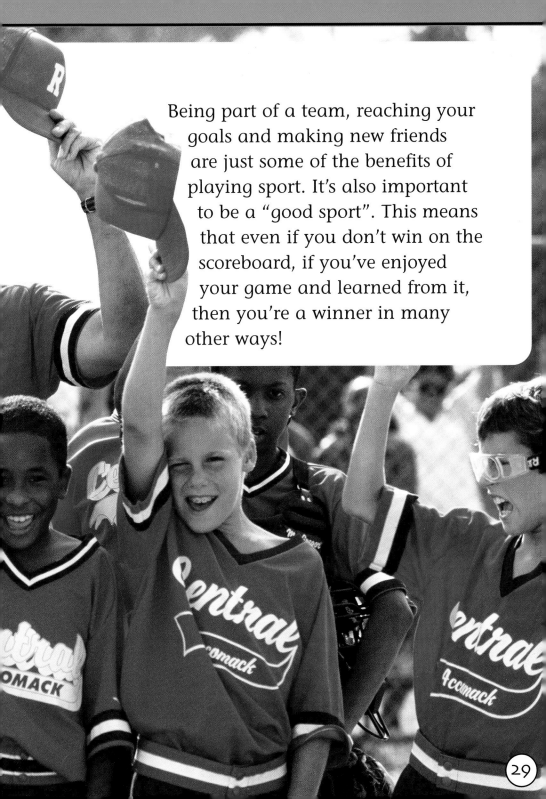

Being part of a team, reaching your goals and making new friends are just some of the benefits of playing sport. It's also important to be a "good sport". This means that even if you don't win on the scoreboard, if you've enjoyed your game and learned from it, then you're a winner in many other ways!

Glossary

agility – the ability to move quickly and easily. Many athletes train to improve their agility, especially those who play ball sports such as basketball and tennis.

disqualify – to stop someone from taking part in an activity, often a sporting event. Athletes are usually disqualified for breaking a rule or for starting a race early.

motivation – eagerness and interest in an activity. Training and practising for a sport is hard work so athletes need motivation to keep pushing themselves towards their goals.

physiology – the scientific study of living things, their body parts and how they work. Exercise physiology is the study of how exercise affects the body and how athletes can use their bodies to gain the best results.

podium – a small platform on which the winners of an event accept their medals. The person in first place is positioned higher than the person in second place, who is positioned slightly higher than the person in third place.

rookie – an athlete in his or her first year of playing for a professional sports team

self-esteem – the confidence in yourself and your abilities

sponsor – a person or a company that pays for equipment and other expenses that an athlete might have

Index

Bibliography

LaBlanc, Michael L. and Richard Henshaw. *The World Encyclopedia of Soccer*. Gale Research Inc., 1994.

Lewis, Michael and United States Soccer Federation, Inc. *Soccer for Dummies*. IDG Books Worldwide, Inc., 2000.

Miller, Shannon and Nancy Ann Richardson. *Winning Every Day*. Bantam Books, 1998.

Owen, Ed. *Playing and Coaching Wheelchair Basketball*. University of Illinois Press, 1982.

Research Starters

1 If you could choose to take part in one of the sports mentioned in this book which one would it be? Research which national or international events are held for this sport. In which event would you most like to participate? Why?

2 Set a sporting goal that you would like to achieve. Now make a weekly training schedule that you can follow to best achieve your goal. Ask someone else for feedback on your schedule.

3 Find out what kind of responsibilities a coach has. Which responsibilities do you think are the most important?

4 The news article on page 17 shows Louise Sauvage winning the wheelchair division of the Boston Marathon in 1998 and 1999. Research the history of this event and find out more about winners in other divisions of the race.